Montana Fish Species

Game Fish & Panfish

Billy Grinslott & Kinsey Marie Books

ISBN - 9781965098820

Chubs and Shiners are two types of minnows that are considered panfish. There are several types of shiners and chubs. Many people will use them as bate to catch larger fish. Here's a list of some. Redside shiner, Spottail shiner. Golden shiner, Lake chub, and Utah chub.

Northern pikeminnows are voracious predators, consuming millions of young salmon and steelhead annually in the river systems. They are managed through a sport-reward fishery program that pays anglers to remove them, to reduce their population. Anglers are paid to catch and turn in pikeminnows. They can grow up to 35 inches in length and 15 pounds in weight and can live at least 11 years.

The Green Sunfish is blue green in color. It has yellow flecks on both its scales and some parts of its sides. The Green Sunfish also has broken blue stripes which is why some people confuse it with the Bluegill. Green Sunfish are very adaptable, they can live in any body of water that has vegetation or weeds. Green sunfish are opportunistic feeders, consuming insects, small fish, and other invertebrates.

Mottled sculpins are small, bottom-dwelling fish with a flattened body shape, large pectoral fins, and a unique camouflage pattern, often found in clear, fast-flowing waters with rocky substrates, and they are known for their ambush hunting tactics. Sculpins have very large mouths and can swallow items nearly as large as themselves.

The bluegill also considered a sunfish is the most popular fish to fish for. They are called pan fish because they are about the size of a frying pan. Bluegills love to eat insects and bugs. They have good vision and rely on their keen eyesight to feed. Three types in this group are the Bluegill, Sunfish, and Pumpkinseed.

The Pumpkinseed is also known as pond perch, sun perch, and punky's sunfish. It can be found in numerous lakes, ponds, and rivers. It is their body shape resembling the seed of a pumpkin, that inspired their name. Pumpkinseed sunfish have speckles on their orangish colored sides and back, with a yellow to orange belly and chest.

The Rock Bass is not actually a bass but a member of the sunfish family. The biggest Rock Bass ever caught on record weighs about three pounds and was a little over one foot long. Rock bass prefer waters with rocky vegetated areas, that's how they got their name. Rock bass can be found in the Tongue River drainage of southeastern Montana.

There are two main types of crappies. The white crappie and the black crappie. They are also members of the sunfish family. The difference between the white and black crappie is one has dark spots and the other has dark lines and is lighter in color. The white crappie has six dorsal fin spines, whereas the black crappie has eight dorsal fin spines. The white crappie can grow bigger and more of the bigger white crappie are caught in North America.

The Warmouth is a member of the Rock Bass, Green Sunfish and Bluegill family. They can survive in low oxygen environments while other fish cannot. Warmouth can thrive in muddy water, when other fish can't. Warmouth are often confused with rock bass. The difference between the two is in the anal fin: warmouth have three spines on the anal fin ray and rock bass have six spines.

The two most famous perches are the common perch and the yellow perch. The yellow perch has a brilliant greenish yellow color with orange fins. The yellow perch is the biggest one and can grow to a size of 18 inches. It's also known as the jumbo perch. The other type of perch is the white perch.

White Bass range in color from a silvery white to a pale green. Their backs are mostly black, while their sides and belly are pale with stripes running along them. White Bass are related to Striped Bass and called wipers. White bass are found in the Missouri River below Fort Peck Dam and the lower Yellowstone River. The largest white bass caught in Montana weighed 6.72 pounds.

In Montana, you're likely to find Goldeye fish in the lower Missouri and Yellowstone rivers, or in Fort Peck Reservoir. Goldeye fish typically average around 12 inches in length and weigh about 1 pound but can grow up to 20 inches long. Their most distinctive feature is their yellow or gold-colored eyes. Their yellow or gold-colored eyes are adapted for low-light conditions and allows them to see when the water is darker. Goldeye are also known as mooneye. The largest Goldeye fish caught in Montana weighed 3.18 pounds.

The largemouth bass is the most sought-after bass in North America. Largemouth bass live in just about every lake in North America. They have great hearing and can hear a crayfish crawling on the bottom of the lake. The largest largemouth bass caught in Montana was a 9.575-pound, 22.5-inches long.

Smallmouth bass have a smaller mouth than the largemouth bass. They also have different markings and are lighter in color. They prefer living in colder water. They are typically found in the northern states in America because the water is cooler. The current world record smallmouth is an 11-pound, 15-ounce fish caught in Dale Hollow Lake. They can be found in over 180 lakes, reservoirs, and rivers, especially in the eastern portion of Montana. The largest smallmouth bass caught in Montana weighed 8.4 pounds, Length 22.4 inches.

Whitefish are related to salmon and trout. They are known for their deep-bodied, silvery appearance and are a major part of the lake's ecosystem. They typically grow to 17-22 inches and range from 1.5-4 pounds. Whitefish are a popular and valuable commercial fish, generating income for commercial fisheries. Whitefish are also known as, whiting, and shad. The largest lake whitefish caught in Montana weighed 10.46 pounds and was 27 inches long.

Montana has one species of gar, the shortnose gar. The Gar got its name because of its long mouth that looks like an alligator's mouth. The alligator gar is one of the biggest freshwater fish growing up to 10 feet long. The world record for a catch was set at 327 pounds. In Montana, you'll find the shortnose gar primarily in the Missouri River dredge cuts downstream of Fort Peck Dam, the Yellowstone River and other large rivers, quiet pools, backwaters, and oxbow lakes. The Montana state record for a shortnose gar is a 35-inch, 7.41-pound fish.

Male freshwater drum make a rumbling or grunting sound by contracting muscles along their air bladder walls. They have large, ivory-like ear bones that can be up to an inch in diameter, which Native Americans used as necklaces or bracelets and sometimes referred to as the lucky stones. Freshwater drum are primarily bottom feeders, spending much of their time near the bottom of lakes and rivers in search of food. The largest freshwater drum caught in Montana weighed 21.59 pounds and 29.5 inches long.

Buffalo Fish are sometimes confused with carp. Buffalo fish have a downward-facing mouth, capable of sucking bits of food out of the silt and sand on the bottom. They have broad bodies, blunt heads, and silvery gray or brown scales. Buffalo fish are members of the suckerfish family. The largest Bigmouth Buffalo caught in Montana weighed 57.75 pounds, Length 40.7 inches.

Carp have long been an important food fish to humans. Carp are bottom feeders for the most part and their mouth is made like a suction cup, so they can suck food off the bottom. Carp are good for a lake because they help clean the bottom of the lake. Carp can tolerate a wide range of water temperatures and low oxygen levels, allowing them to survive in a variety of habitats. The largest carp caught in Montana weighed 40.27 pounds.

The black bullhead and yellow bullhead are part of the catfish family. They usually only grow to about 10 inches long. They use their whiskers to help find food. The bullhead is the most common member of the catfish family. Bullheads live in the water containing low oxygen levels. They can survive on low oxygen areas, where other fish can't.

There are a couple different types of catfish in Montana, the channel and the stonecat. The Channel Catfish are the most fished catfish species with around 8 million anglers fishing for them per year. Channel Catfish have very few teeth and swallow their food whole. Channel catfish live in freshwater rivers, lakes, streams, and ponds. Catfish can live in low oxygen water, like bullheads. The largest channel catfish caught in Montana weighed 35.18 pounds.

Montana is home to nine species of sucker fish. The bigmouth buffalo, smallmouth buffalo, river carpsucker, short- head redhorse, largescale sucker, longnose sucker, blue sucker, plains sucker, and white sucker. The largescale sucker holds the state record at 6.72-pound and was 25.25 inches long.

Redhorse fishes are part of the sucker family and are known for their bottom-facing mouths and fleshy lips which they use to suck food off the bottom. Redhorse has large, molar-like throat teeth that are an adaptation for crushing the shells of mollusks. redhorses construct nests in clean gravel, using their tails to sweep and their mouths to carry rocks or move materials with their heads.

Lake Sturgeons have sharp spines on their back, so be careful when handling them. Instead of scales, sturgeon skin is covered in bony plates called scutes, which can be very sharp on young sturgeon. Sturgeons have been around since the dinosaur days. Sturgeons mostly live in large, freshwater lakes and rivers. Their average lifespan is 50 to 60 years. The largest sturgeon caught in Montana is a 96-pound white sturgeon, Length 75 inches.

The sauger is part of the walleye family. There are 2 different types of saugers. The normal sauger and the suageye. The saugeye is a mix of the sauger and walleye. The suageye have white eyes just like the walleye. The sauger and suageye are smaller than the walleye. They are particularly common in rivers like the Yellowstone and Missouri. The largest sauger caught in Montana weighed 8.805 pounds and measured 28.2 inches long.

The walleye got its name because of its white looking eyes. Their eyes collect light, even in low light conditions. This means they can see in the dark. Because they can see in the dark, they mostly feed at night. During the daytime their eyes are very sensitive, so they usually head for deeper water or shady places. Walleye like to live in cooler water and are normally found in the upper part of North America. Walleye are a popular sport fish in Montana, especially in the eastern part of the state. The largest walleye caught in Montana weighed 18.02 pounds, measured 32.25 inches long.

The Northern Pike is one of the most sought-after fish for anglers. It got its name because it likes to live in cooler water mainly in the northern states of North America. The northern pike is a very aggressive predator. They don't like to live in groups with other fish, they are very territorial and like to live alone. Their behavior is closely affected by weather conditions. Due to widespread introductions Northern Pike are now a common gamefish statewide. The largest northern pike caught in Montana weighed 37.5 pounds.

The tiger muskie is a cross between the northern pike and muskie. They grow larger and faster than normal muskies and northern pikes. The tiger muskie got its name because it has tiger like stripes. Tiger Muskies are very rare and hard to catch. Ackley Lake and Deadman Basin are known for their tiger muskellunge populations, with Ackley Lake even holding the IGFA all-tackle length world record for the species. The largest tiger muskie caught in Montana was a 45.2-inch fish which is a IGFA All-Tackle Length World Record.

Mature Golden trout have a deep olive-green back that fades to bright gold on the sides, a vibrant red-orange lateral line, and black speckles near the tail. Golden trout are native to the remote waters at elevations of 6,000 to 10,000 feet. The largest golden trout caught in Montana weighed 5.43 pounds and was 23.5 inches long.

The Cutthroat trout is Montana's state fish. The cutthroat's name comes from the bright red or orange slash-like markings under their jaws. There are several subspecies of cutthroat trout, including the coastal, Yellowstone, and Lahontan cutthroat. They inhabit a variety of cold, freshwater environments, including small streams, rivers, and lakes. The largest Cutthroat trout caught in Montana weighed 16 pounds, was 32 inches long.

Bull trout thrive in cold, clean, and complex aquatic habitats, with water temperatures ideally below 55°F. Some bull trout are anadromous, meaning they migrate from freshwater to saltwater for part of their life cycle, and then return to freshwater to spawn. Bull trout usually grow to a common length of around 25 inches, with the maximum reported length being 40.5 inches. The largest bull trout caught in Montana weighed 25 pounds and 10 ounces, and was 37 inches long.

Yellowstone cutthroat trout, a native species in Montana, are distinguished by prominent red slashes on their lower jaws, large black spots, and orange to drab coloration. They inhabit relatively clear, cold streams, rivers, and lakes. They typically measure from 6 to 30 inches long when they reach maturity. The largest Yellowstone Cutthroat Trout caught in Montana was 28 inches.

Brown trout can live up to 20 years. Brown trout have higher tolerance for warmer waters than either brook or rainbow trout. Brown trout can be found on almost every continent except Antarctica, and many can be found living in the ocean. The largest brown trout caught in Montana, and a new state record, weighed in at 32.43 pounds and was 37 inches long.

The Arctic grayling is one of the most beautiful freshwater fishes. Its most striking physical feature is the large, sail like dorsal or backfin. The Arctic grayling comes in a wide array of colors. Their color can vary from stream to stream. The sides of the body, fins and head can be freckled with spots. They can grow to be 30 inches long and weigh up to 8.4 pounds. They can travel more than 100 miles in one year. The largest Arctic grayling caught in Montana weighed 2 pounds, 10 ounces and measured 18 inches long.

In Montana, the primary salmon species you'll find are landlocked sockeye salmon, known as kokanee. These are the non-anadromous form of sockeye salmon, meaning they don't migrate to the ocean. They live their entire lives in freshwater lakes and reservoirs. The largest kokanee salmon caught in Montana weighed 7.85 pounds and was 26.8 inches long.

Chinook also known as the king salmon are the most widespread Salmon in North America. Chinook salmon are hatch in freshwater streams and rivers then migrate out to the saltwater environment of the ocean to feed and grow. Chinook salmon are the largest of the Pacific Ocean salmon, that's how they got the name king salmon. The largest Chinook salmon caught in Montana weighed 32.62 pounds.

The lake trout is one of the biggest of the trout family. The biggest lake trout caught was 72 pounds. Lake trout like to live in lakes that are deep. They like being in the cool water in the deep parts of a lake. They have been reported to live up to 70 years in some Canadian lakes. Montana State record is a 42.69-pound fish measuring 42.5 inches long.

Fun Facts About Montana Fish

1 - The blackspotted cutthroat trout was designated the state fish on February 10, 1977.

2 - Rainbow and Brown Trout were introduced to Montana waters, and are now widely dispersed.

3 - The lake sturgeon is a giant, with some weighing over 100 pounds and living over 150 years.

4 - Whitefish are a popular native gamefish, known for their abundance and willingness to take bait or artificial flies.

5 - Montana is known for its world-class trout fishing, with many river options and trip packages.

6 - Yellowstone Cutthroat Trout are the most widespread native trout and dominant fish species throughout Montana.

7 - Montana holds the records for these largest fish caught, Chinook Salmon, Cisco, Coho Salmon, and Common Carp.

Author Page

Billy Grinslott & Kinsey Marie Books

Copyright, All Rights Reserved

ISBN – 9781965098820

Thanks

9 781965 098820